Worcester

in old picture postcards

by
Brian R. Owen

European Library – Zaltbommel/Netherlands

GB ISBN 90 288 5402 9 / CIP

© 1992 European Library – Zaltbommel/Netherlands

No part of this book may be reproduced in any form, by print, photoprint, microfilm or any other means, without written permission from the publisher.

INTRODUCTION

The illustrations in this book span the years from about 1880 to 1930, encompassing what is usually referred to as the 'Golden Age' of the picture postcard — that semi-mythical time, when for the price of a halfpenny postage stamp you could drop a postcard into the letter box at nine o'clock in the morning bearing the message, 'See you in the Cross at four this afternoon' and be safe in the knowledge that your friend on the other side of Worcester would receive it in good time to keep the rendezvous. Four postal deliveries a day — those were the days! How often we say it, and how easy it is to believe, when looking at old postcard views of Worcester! People and places frozen in time and, indeed, the City of Worcester as represented in the views, has a timeless quality about it. At first glance very little has changed and then one begins to notice little differences...!

Of course time never stands still; Worcester has changed and always will change. During the fifty or so years covered by the illustrations in this book, the City and its inhabitants altered to a remarkable degree.

Let's consider for a start changes brought about by technology. In 1880 Great Britain still led the world in technical achievement, even though the lead was beginning to slip to competitors, and it was many years before the effect showed. By 1930 we looked to the USA for the lead in most things technical.

The most significant technical change was undoubtedly the spread of the internal combustion engine from about 1900. By the end of our period, the motorcar was bringing freedom to the working man and his family, but it had already sown the seeds of traffic chaos in the old city centre! Railways, pre-eminent in 1880, were by 1930 losing out as bulk movers of goods and people to the motorcar, the motor bus and the lorry. The River Severn, the 'corridor of the west', once the busiest river in the world, had already been pushed into decline by the railways; the development of road transport was the final straw, even if by a strange irony, its decline was temporarily halted by the petroleum trade up to Worcester! In 1910 the first powered aeroplane seen in Worcester, a flimsy Bleriot, shuddered into the air from Pitchcroft to herald in another new form of transport — one which (fortunately?) was not to come to maturity at Worcester, even if the city did later possess. at Perdiswell, Britain's first Local Authority Airport!

Worcester was equally quick off the mark with gas lighting (from 1818) and during the 1880s, the perfected incandescent gaslights began to be fitted inside city homes, just in time to be superseded by electricity, although for a time both systems ran side by side. How much more convenient was a gas stove than the old kitchen range! And an electric cooker... well! Electricity, available in Worcester from 1894, made possible the telephone, the cinema (Worcester's first was the Apollo, opened in Park Street in 1911), a weekly institution by the late 1920s; and radio which would become a national pastime during the next decade. Electric tramcars came and went in Worcester within our period, a sacrificial victim to the motorcar!

New, technology-based industries appeared in Worcester — engineering to rival or replace the old craft-based industries of porcelain manufacture and gloving. By 1930 the city could count amongst its wares: machine tools, metal castings, mining equipment, metal fastenings, incinerators and water-cooling equipment, railway signals and tin cans.

Worcester's citizens changed too in their expectations and attitudes. Advances in medicine and public health reduced infant mortality and increased life expectancy from those levels accepted as normal in 1880. Much social change was brought about by enlightened legislation, particularly in the realm of education. By the 1880s, most of the children who had previously 'slipped through the net' were rounded up as a result of the 1870 Education Act. The denominational and Board Schools working side by side, did sterling work in the city. The 1891 Act provided free Elementary Education and in 1914, the minimum school leaving age was raised to fourteen. Worcester had already made provision for boys and girls to go on to Secondary Education.

Education broadened horizons. Roles and class structure began to be questioned and then threatened. The years 1890 to 1910 saw the early development of the trades union movement and a big change in the role of women as they went into teaching and office work. And then came the First World War – 'the war to end wars' – and nothing was ever the same again. Values and attitudes once confidently taken for granted, were completely overthrown, as family and community were torn apart by tragic loss. Those at home coped with food shortage, rationing and queuing, foreshadowing those of 1939-1945. Manpower losses to the armed forces brought women to the fore. In Worcester they manned offices, took fares on the trams, laboured in the Blackpole munitions factory and on the land surrounding the city. Women's war service could not be ignored, neither any longer could their demands for suffrage. In 1918, with women forming the majority of the population, they were finally given the vote.

Now, however, women expected more than household drudgery, and their male partners, those soldiers who had returned from the war expected 'homes fit for heroes'. The result was legislation to provide decent housing for the working classes. Worcester met the challenge with a programme of new estate construction – in 1922 at Northwick, followed by schemes at Tolladine, Brickfields, Bromwich Road and Barneshall. This enabled the 'clearance' of tightly-packed, often squalid areas in the city centre which would completely change its character and which would continue until the 1960s.

In reality therefore, a turmoil of change took place beneath the peaceful façade of Worcester throughout the 'Golden Age' of the picture postcard. To attempt to show something of this, photographs have been included here which are not postcards, but which were taken for various other reasons. They include several from a remarkable series taken for the City Sanitary Inspector to demonstrate housing conditions prevalent in certain city centre areas during the late 1920s.

All of the postcards and photographs in this book are from the collection of the Worcester City Museum, based in Foregate Street. Collectively, the illustrations I have chosen do not tell any particular story, but each individually does have something to say about the city's past. I hope therefore, that this will be a book to be picked up and 'dipped into' at any page. Hopefully, it will stir the memories of those old enough to remember, and perhaps stimulate the curiosity of those who are not, or who are (like me) relative newcomers to Worcester. Everything in the city is the way it is for an historical reason and should not lightly be taken for granted.

We are forever indebted to those who photographically recorded the city, whatever their original motivation may have been. Many of the photographers are alas unknown, including those who took views for the large postcard publishers. Amongst the local photographers whose work is known to be represented here, are: T. Bennett & Son, W.W. Dowty, Horace Dudley, Norman May, A.D. McGuirk and Percy Parsons. Long may their successors continue the invaluable work.

Acknowledgments

My grateful thanks are due to the Leisure Services Committee of Worcester City Council for making available the City Museum photograph collection; to my colleagues at the City Museum for their never failing interest and support and, in particular, Tim Bridges for reading the draft; to the staff of Worcester City Library and, most of all, to my wife Gill who typed the draft and coped uncomplainingly with all my textual alterations.

March 1992   Brian Owen

1. One must begin any tour of Worcester at the river for on a crossing point of the Severn, the ancient city was born. From the river bridge one obtains a perfect view of the Cathedral, in what must be one of the most photographed views in Britain! On the left of this postcard dating from about 1930, is Dent, Allcroft & Co's factory, which until its closure in 1959, was one of the largest manufacturers of leather gloves in a city once renowned for them. The glove factory in its turn, was housed in the building of the original Worcester Porcelain Works, founded in 1751.

WORCESTER CATHEDRAL AND BRIDGE OVER SEVERN.

2. Worcester has had several river bridges. Wooden structures were replaced by a stone bridge in 1313, several hundred yards upstream from the present site. By the 1760s, this bridge was a source of some embarrassment to the City Council, whose role was to maintain it against the depredations of flood, tide and clumsy boatmen and so an elegant, new bridge was built to the design of John Gwynne. Only a few years after it opened to traffic in 1781, agitation began to have it widened! This finally happened in 1847. An extra eight feet of road width was obtained by removal of pavements and the addition of new cast iron pavements and railings hung out on cantilevers. Work on the widening was carried out by Edward Leader Williams, the local engineer, and the results were strangely elegant! In this form the river bridge stayed until the 1930s.

3. On the other side of the river bridge is South Quay and this view, taken from the bridge parapet, dates from 1892. The warehouses on the quayside were mainly operated by hop factors, but seed and feed merchants and mineral water manufacturers were also active. The tall chimney stack belongs to Dent, Allcroft's Glove factory. The railway line alongside the quayside, came off the Worcester to Hereford line at the viaduct further upstream and in 1860 was intended to be an important rail link to Diglis Dock. Unfortunately, the Cathedral authorities had a change of heart and refused to allow the line to pass under the Cathedral. It therefore terminated on South Quay.

4. From the late eighteenth century attempts were made to improve the navigation of the River Severn, to allow vessels free access up to and beyond Worcester without being troubled by tides and shallow water. An attempt sponsored by the City and entrepreneurs of Worcester in 1836 was defeated in Parliament but led to the setting up of the Severn Commission, whose next attempt in 1842 met with success. The plan was to increase the depth of water by six feet up to Worcester by constructing a series of weirs and locks. Resident engineer was Edward Leader Williams of Worcester. Diglis Lock and Weir was one of the series, comprising a weir 400 feet long and two parallel locks of different sizes. Diglis Lock was opened to traffic in 1844 and this view dates from the 1890s. Notice the steam tug heading downstream out of the lock, and the salmon fishing nets drying on the banks of the island.

5. The Severn was fished for all varieties, but the most important was the salmon. By the eighteenth century, there was a well-established fishing community occupying cottages beneath the west end of the cathedral and in Frog Lane (Severn Street). From the mid-nineteenth century, legislation restricted commercial fishing and the trade went into decline. Net fishing on the upper Severn officially ended by Act of Parliament in 1929. The salmon net could be 100-200 yards long and was 'shot out' across the river from a punt in a radius from a fixed point on the river bank. When the punt reached the bank again, the net and its catch were hauled in. The view dated about 1905, shows nets drying at Diglis Weir, a favoured fishing location.

6. A steam tug bringing a mixed tow of narrowboats and a timber barge upriver out of Diglis Lock in about 1908. Moored to the left of the tug is a Droitwich salt trow. From 1771, when the Droitwich Canal was opened, until the early years of this century, the little salt trows made regular trips right down to Bristol laden with salt, and returned mainly with corn.

7. The steamship 'Atalanta' transshipping her cargo to narrowboats at South Quay during the 1890s. Built at Bristol in 1894, 'Atalanta' was purchased the following year by the Severn and Canal Carrying Company. She was used mainly for coastal work, but often traded up to Worcester with cargoes of iron or copper ore destined for the industrial Midlands. 'Atalanta' was converted to internal combustion in 1916 and sold off in 1939.

THE PROMENADE, WORCESTER

8. The Promenade at the river's edge seen from inside the Cathedral West Garden in a postcard of about 1910. Still a favourite Sunday afternoon walk, the Promenade is believed to have, as its foundation, old river barges filled with rubble and sunk in the mid-nineteenth century. At the left of the picture is All Saints' Church, one of the medieval city churches, rebuilt during the eighteenth century. To the right of it are the buildings and chimney of Dent, Allcroft's glove factory, and the spire of St. Andrew's Church. The ruins of monastic buildings can be seen on the right of the picture.

9. Worcester has had several 'alternative' river crossing points Amongst them was the Cathedral Ferry, which originated for the use of monks at the Priory to cross to the lands they worked on the west bank of the Severn. After the dissolution of the monasteries under Henry VIII, operation of the ferry passed to the Dean and Chapter of the Cathedral and was subject to many strict regulations. As a boy Worcester's famous composer, Edward Elgar, was a regular user of the ferry, crossing the river to get to his school at Lower Wick. The Cathedral Ferry lapsed during the 1950s, but has recently been successfully revived.

10. Worcester Cathedral from the Severn, a photographic view posted in 1913. Although the Diocese of Worcester was founded in 680 A.D., the present Cathedral building with its adjoining monastery, was commenced in 1084. The tower collapsed in 1175 and rebuilding was not completed until 1374. The monastery was dissolved in 1540. The exterior of the Cathedral as seen in this view, is largely the result of restoration carried out under the direction of A.E. Perkins and Sir Gilbert Scott between 1855 and 1875. The line of the medieval city wall can be followed at the river edge and the Water Gate, the last surviving city gate (to the right of the photograph), dates from 1378.

11. The Cathedral and Deanery in a view dating from the turn of the century. The Deanery or 'Old Palace' as it is known today, was until 1842 the Bishop's residence, along with Hartlebury Castle. In 1846 the Dean and Chapter of the Cathedral purchased it for the use of the Dean and demolished the old deanery on College Green, together with the Guesten Hall. In more recent years the Old Palace has been used as diocesan offices and a club. The main structure of the building dates from the thirteenth century, but considerable alterations were carried out during the eighteenth century.

12. Worcester Cathedral from the north-east, in a Frith's postcard view of the late 1890s. It shows to full advantage the Lady Chapel added to the Cathedral during the thirteenth century. So successful was it, that the whole of the quire was rebuilt in the same style, completely transforming the Cathedral. The east window was rebuilt in the lancet style of the thirteenth century in 1864. The iron railings, seen enclosing the Cathedral in this view, fell victim to the salvage campaign of the Second World War.

Ruins of the Guesten Hall, Worcester.

Photo. Bennett & Sons.

13. The ruins of the Cathedral Guesten Hall. The Guesten Hall, built in the fourteenth century, was used for the entertainment of guests to the monastery and access to it was via a passageway off the cloisters. The Hall survived until 1862, when because of its dilapidated state, it was demolished except for one wall which was allowed to remain as a picturesque ruin. The roof of the hall was re-used at the new Holy Trinity Church at Shrub Hill. When in 1969 Holy Trinity too was demolished, the roof was again saved, this time by the Avoncroft Museum of Buildings where it can now be seen. This postcard view from about 1900 is one of a set photographed by T. Bennett & Sons of Worcester and published by Simes Department Store in High Street.

Castle House and the Hostel, King's School, Worcester.

Pub. by Photo Tourists Association, Turnham Green W.

14. College Green south side, in a postcard view dating from 1905. The eighteenth century houses were built for the Cathedral canons and some of them incorporate remains of monastic outbuildings. The houses are virtually unchanged today, but the large trees and iron railings on the left have gone.

15. The precincts of the monastery based on the Cathedral were entered by the Edgar Tower, shown in this postcard of circa 1898. It was probably built during the fourteenth century and was originally known as 'Priory Gate' or 'St. Mary's Gate'. The name 'Edgar Tower' derives from a statue, very ancient and worn, of Edgar, King of England A.D. 959-975, above the gateway in a niche, just visible in the picture. In the two eroded niches, one each side of the windows, were statues of Edgar's wives. Soon after this picture was taken, the exterior of the Tower was restored and the niches reinstated. A replacement 'King Edgar' was inserted into the niche and the wives replaced by figures of St. Oswald and St. Wulstan.

16. Until the 1960s Worcester could boast the only surviving Cathedral Lich Gate. It stood a hundred yards or so to the north of the Cathedral altar, on a site where a hotel now stands. Lich Street, on the other side of the gate, contained some of the oldest houses in the city, which, although picturesque, had for very many years been divided into tenements and had declined into near squalor. The whole area was demolished in a redevelopment which helped make Worcester a byword for urban desecration! The illustration from a postcard by Frith & Co of the 1890s, is taken from the Lich Street side of the gate, looking through to the Cathedral. On the left of the 'alley' stands the 'Punch Bowl' Inn.

17. The Guildhall in the High Street is traditionally the administrative centre of Worcester and is the base for the Mayor and officers of Worcester City Council. It has been for centuries the focal point for civic ceremony and was also a Court of Justice for both City and County until 1838, when the County Court moved to the Shire Hall. The original Guildhall was a timber-framed building which was replaced by the present edifice in 1721-1723, built to the design of Thomas White, the celebrated Worcester architect, at a cost of £3,727. Plans to demolish the elegant Georgian structure during the 1870s in favour of a grandiose new Guildhall were fortunately shelved and a restoration was carried out instead under Sir Gilbert Scott and Henry Rowe, the City Architect. The postcard illustration dates from about 1910.

18. The shop of Daniel Mitchell at 75 High Street. Mitchell was listed in the trade directories as a 'complete house furnisher, oil and lamp merchant and boot and shoe factor'. He was in business from about 1860 until the early 1890s. This building still exists.

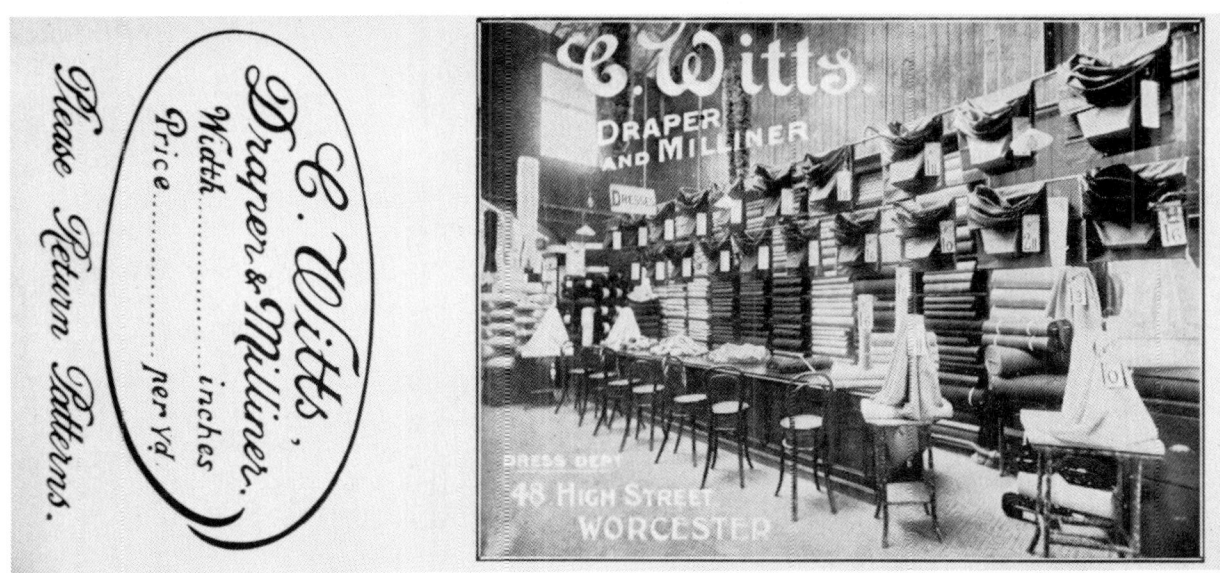

19. The dress department of C. Witts' drapery store at 48 High Street, as featured in a fabric sample card of the 1920s. Drapery shops flourished during the nineteenth century, some becoming early department stores such as Simes' and Turley's of Worcester. The introduction of cheap factory clothing early this century however, brought about a steady decline in home dressmaking. Even a small draper's and haberdasher's held an enormous range of items apart from fabrics: pins, needles, buckles, buttons, elastics, threads, trimmings of all kinds, collars and cuffs, boot laces, corsetry, underwear and nightwear, gloves and stockings could all be found. The shops prided themselves on the personal attention they provided and were rewarded by strong customer loyalty. C. Witts' were founded in 1904 and later had a shop in St. Johns.

20. The Market Hall entrance in High Street circa 1930. The Market Hall was completed in 1804 on the site of the King's Head Inn, almost directly opposite the Guildhall. All that remains of it in the High Street now is the fine clock, given in 1849 by the Mayor Richard Padmore. A Worcester guidebook of 1855 states 'The general appearance of the building on entering... reminds the visitor of the transept of the Great Exhibition of 1851 of which it is a copy; the centre of the roof is of glass, the sides of corrugated iron, the whole being supported by iron pillars.' Even 150 years after the Great Exhibition, every shopping mall built in Britain seemingly has to be a pseudo-Crystal Palace. I wonder why?

21. The Market Hall ran between High Street and the Shambles and faced the meat market opposite, which still exists. A 'wing' of the market, opened in 1881, led through to Pump Street. Apart from farm produce, the market had stalls selling various household items and clothing. Perhaps the most famous was Sigley's China Store, seen here at sale time in 1910. In the early 1920s, Sigley's became Winkle's and even though the market was redeveloped in the 1960s as a shopping arcade, the atmosphere of the old market still remains with Pratley's China Store, the direct descendant of Sigley's and Winkle's.

22. Many English towns and cities have their 'Shambles' or meat markets. This is Worcester's, from a postcard photograph of the late 1890s. The 'Butcher's Arms' closed at the end of the 1950s and on its site is now a chain store. Many of the butchers' shops had their own slaughterhouses at the rear of the premises up until the 1930s. But the Shambles was not all butchers; also located there was the china shop of Sigley's (later Pratley's) and the much-loved ironmongers, J & F Hall, on the corner of Church Street.

23. One of the oldest established businesses in Worcester was that of J & F Hall Ltd, which had its origins in the eighteenth century. From their premises in a superb half-timbered building, dating from the sixteenth century, situated on the corner of the Shambles adjacent to St. Swithun's Church, Hall's dealt in a vast range of ironmongery and hardware, as well as providing a plumbing and sanitary engineering service. Unfortunately, Hall's building was demolished in the mid-1960s.

24. The Arcade Cinema stood in St. Swithin Street, its building now occupied by a chain chemist, and it opened in 1912, a year after Worcester's first cinema, Evans' Picture Palace (later the Apollo) opened its doors in a converted chapel in Park Street. The photograph, by W.W. Dowty of Broad Street, Worcester, dates from the early 1920s, when seats could be had for prices ranging from 9d to 1/6d (4p to 8p)! The Arcade ceased to operate in the early 1930s.

25. Burden's Bakery at 8 St. Swithin Street, which when the photograph was taken, was the largest bakery business in Worcester. The business was established in 1891 and soon had branches in St. Johns, the Tything and in Sidbury. All kinds of bread were baked as well as every variety of plain and fancy cake.

26. This interesting photograph shows St. Swithin Street from the Cross and would appear to have been taken in 1890, for in that year St. Swithin Street was widened by demolition of the shops visible on its north (left hand) side. The posters on 'Goldrings' shop read, 'Removing the Cross.' The building on the right hand side was in 1890 occupied by the Central Temperance Hotel and Restaurant. Notice the boy selling newspapers.

27. The Cross has for centuries been regarded as the centre of the City of Worcester and in medieval times a stone cross stood there. The buildings of the Cross are dominated today, as on this postcard of the early 1900s, by the fine tower of St. Nicholas' Church. Originally dating from the twelfth century, St. Nicholas was rebuilt in the early 1730s, possibly by Humphrey Hollins, a local architect. During the mid-nineteenth century, the vicar of St. Nicholas was the Reverend W.H. Havergal, father of the famous writer of hymns, Frances Ridley Havergal. In the centre of the picture, to the right of the Foregate railway bridge, can be seen the Hopmarket, which was rebuilt in 1903-1904.

28. The Cross, looking eastwards in a view which dates from 1904. The electric trams have now arrived, and car No. 3 on the Barbourne route awaits passengers. Behind the tram is the splendid classical façade of Lloyd's Bank, built to the designs of E.W. Elmslie in 1861 and constructed like many of the city centre buildings by Joseph Wood of Worcester. Before its amalgamation, the bank was the headquarters of the Worcester City and County Banking Company, founded in 1840 by a consortium of local businessmen (including Richard Padmore of Hardy and Padmore, ironfounders, and Edward Evans of Hill, Evans & Co, vinegar manufacturers). 'The Golden Cross', next to the bank, was a gentlemen's tailoring business.

29. About eight to ten years separate this view of the Cross from the previous one but in this time electric trams have arrived and great changes have taken place on the east (right hand) side. The Hopmarket and hotel has been rebuilt with an impressive terracotta façade and cupolas. What on the previous card was 'The Golden Cross', a tailoring business operated by Masters & Co, has now been radically altered and faced with stone. From that point on, all the buildings on both sides of St. Swithin Street and extending for some distance along High Street to Church Street beyond where the camera is placed, have new façades, with much use of terracotta and very fine detailing. The next photograph explains what happened...

30. Before 1904 the High Street narrowed considerably towards the Cross end. The buildings on the east side were small and in various stages of decrepitude. The newly formed Worcester Electric Traction Company, in order to obtain the width of road required to construct an electric tram route along the High Street, made considerable cash contributions to have the frontages of the buildings concerned set back. This fascinating photograph taken in 1903, shows the work at a transitional stage. The new frontages have been built, but some of the old shops remain to be demolished. The overhead power lines for the trams are in position and the track is being laid. Notice that the policeman wears a 'spiked' helmet, characteristic of the Worcester City Police Force.

31. The west side of the Cross in about 1910. It contrasts strongly with the east side. in that it has no large impressive buildings, but is made up of an interesting 'jumble' of shops, mainly ladies' and gents' outfitters, including in the centre, the aforementioned J. Masters & Co., who early in this century moved 'across the Cross' into new premises. Most of the buildings shown still survive although many of the façades have been altered.

32. The Cross decorated with a triumphal arch and masses of flags for the visit of HRH The Duke of York (later King George V) in 1894, to lay the foundation stone of the Victoria Institute. Framed in the arch is Turley's store, established on the west side of the Cross in about 1800. Turley's was a dressmaker and milliner, a drapery and haberdashery and also a household furnisher. It also operated as an undertaker and ran a mourning wear department. Dresses were made and furniture constructed, all within the Cross premises. Turley's itself passed away in 1910.

33. St. Nicholas Street, looking towards the Cross from a postcard of about 1910. Trinity Street leads out of the picture on the left hand side and in the corner building were established in 1848 the offices of the Worcester New Gas Light Company, the successors to the company that had brought gaslighting to the city in 1818, only five years after gaslights had first appeared in London. The same building became, in 1888, the headquarters of the Worcester Co-operative Society. Worcester's first telephone exchange was situated in St. Nicholas Street and opened in 1892 with twelve subscribers.

34. Queen Elizabeth's House, also known as Trinity House, photographed in the early 1890s. Traditionally, Queen Elizabeth I addressed the citizens of Worcester from its gallery during her visit in 1575, but the title more likely refers to an endowment made by Queen Elizabeth to the Trinity Almshouses. In 1891 the house was in danger of demolition due to improvements to Trinity Passage, which passed underneath the right hand side of the house. A committee was formed to save it, with the Mayor at its head, and cash was raised to jack up the house and move it bodily to the right a distance of its own length. This considerable feat of engineering was carried out by the Worcester builders Messrs. Bromage and Evans.

35. A splendid photograph of the rear of Queen Elizabeth's House before it was moved in 1891, showing how Trinity Passage passed underneath it. Comparison of this photograph with the previous one demonstrates the result of the move. The house on the left of this photograph can be seen *behind* Queen Elizabeth's House on the previous one.

36. The frontage of Queen Elizabeth's house, again before the move of 1891. The figures on the right are standing in Trinity Passage.

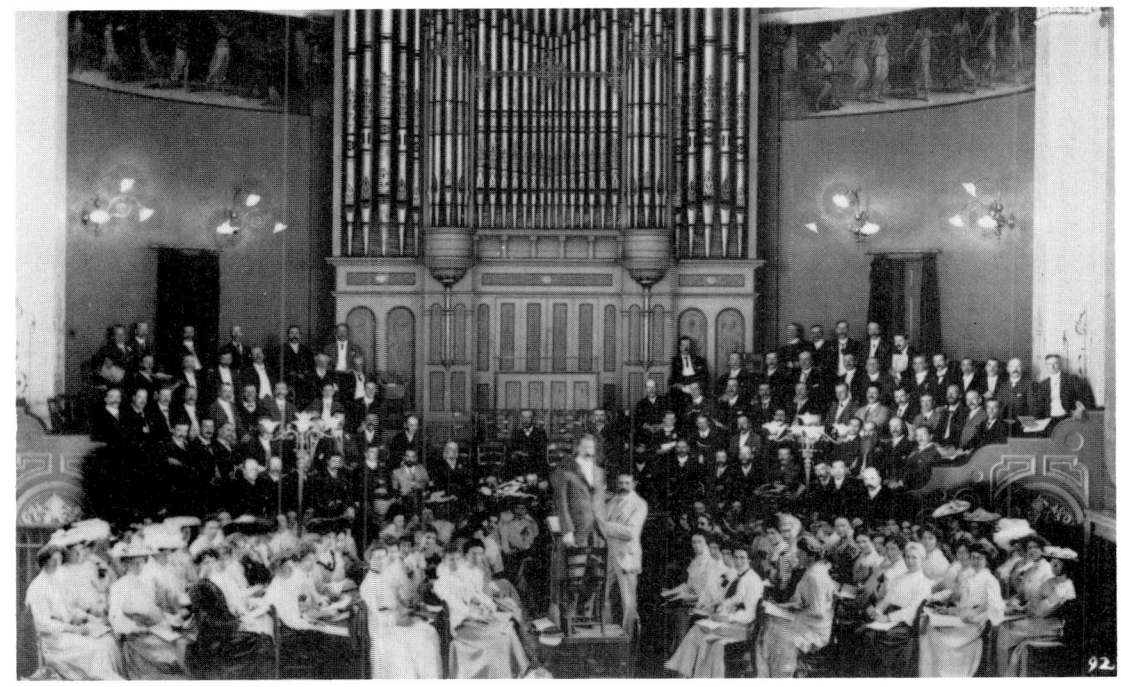

37. Whenever 'lost landmarks' of Worcester are discussed, the Public Hall in the Cornmarket is sure to be mentioned. Dearly loved, no real replacement for it has ever been made. In a city famed for its music, the Public Hall was the venue for music of all kinds, from symphony concerts to minstrel shows. Jenny Lind sang there, Dvorak conducted his own work there and Charles Dickens read there! It was used by schools and by politicians, and for public meetings of all kinds. During the First World War it was the centre for army recruiting drives and during the Second World War it was a Civic Restaurant – the splendid organ by Nicholson of Worcester was apparently ruined by the cooking. The photograph shows the Festival Chorus with Sir Edward Elgar, centre, during the 1905 Three Choirs Festival. During this Festival Elgar was made an Honorary Freeman of the City of Worcester.

38. King Charles' House on the corner of the Cornmarket, was originally the town house of the Berkeley family of Spetchley and was probably built in 1577. Its claim to fame is that it was used by King Charles II as his lodgings during the ill-fated Worcester campaign of 1651, and it was from this house that he made his escape. Unfortunately, the house is greatly changed from its appearance at that time, possibly because a fire at a later date destroyed half of it (out of the picture on the right hand side) and caused a third storey to be removed. The postcard dates from about 1905, when the sign above the door testified to the occupier being Charles Collins, bricklayer and plasterer.

39. A 'conjectural' painting, showing the appearance of King Charles' House in the Cornmarket before it was rebuilt in the 18th century. The artist is E.A. Phipson, whose work is well represented on postcards of Worcester at the turn of the century. The postcard was one of a series issued by Joseph Littlebury's Commandery Press.

40. Nash's House in New Street, from a tinted postcard of about 1905. This was the birthplace of Alderman John Nash (1590-1662), Mayor of Worcester and M.P. for the city in the years before the Civil War. Nash was a cloth merchant and a staunch Parliamentarian. When the wars came, he served as a Captain of Horse. On his death, Nash left a charity in the form of a hospital for the aged. The modern successors to his almshouses still stand behind New Street, a little way along from his house. John Nash's elaborate tomb can be seen in St. Helen's Church in Fish Street.

41. The buildings in Friar Street are amongst the oldest in the city. The Friary which gave the street its name was founded by the Franciscan order in 1235 and the street developed around it. Most of the houses though, date from the late fifteenth or early sixteenth centuries. The house now known as 'Greyfriars' (with the handcart outside it in this view of about 1900) appears however to have no links at all with the Friary. Unfortunately, its early history is unknown, save that it was probably built during the 1470s. At the time this view was taken, Greyfriars was 'multi-occupied' and a row of cottages — 'George's Yard' — stood in what is now its garden.

42. Next to Greyfriars, on the corner of Friar Street and Union Street, originally the site of the Friary, stood the City Gaol. It opened in 1824 and could hold eighty prisoners. One of its best features was a treadmill! Into the gaol, on the Union Street side, was built a 'watchhouse' wherein were based the forerunners of the police. When Worcester City Police Force was formed in 1833, it took over the 'watchhouse' as its headquarters. In 1869 the City Gaol was amalgamated with the County Gaol in Salt Lane (now Castle Street). The City Gaol site was sold to William Laslett, a noted Worcester solicitor and barrister and a great benefactor. He converted the gaol buildings to almshouses and within those forbidding walls, the aged recipients of Laslett's Charity dwelt until 1911, when the gaol was demolished and replaced with a charming development of mock Tudor almshouses around a green.

43. A photograph taken today from the same viewpoint as this postcard of Friar Street by Frith & Co, dated 1911, would show that remarkably little has changed, apart from the façades of the shops. For centuries, Friar Street has been occupied by small tradesmen and retailers. During the eighteenth and early nineteenth centuries, many of them were Quakers or other non-conformists and in this photograph halfway along the street can be seen the entrance, now destroyed, to the Welcome Mission Hall which stood behind the houses. The high wall on the right of the picture was originally the wall of the City Gaol. The crowd of small boys no doubt appeared from nowhere, as soon as the photographer set up his camera!

44. Friar Street in a postcard of 1931. Taken from a similar viewpoint, the photograph makes an interesting comparison with the previous one. The most obvious difference is that on the right hand side the high wall around Laslett's Almshouses, inherited from the old City Gaol, has gone. E. Watts at No. 30 was a hardware store with its origins in a mattress making business of the 1890s.

45. A souvenir postcard of the 'Tudor Coffee House' in Friar Street, dated about 1912. At this time the building was owned by the Cadbury family, of chocolate fame, and operated as a confectioner's with tea room and a restaurant upstairs. The building, originally two houses, dates from the early 1500s and was evidently built for someone fairly wealthy. From the early seventeenth century until the late nineteenth, the right hand half of Tudor House was a tavern – 'The Cross Keys'. The building was purchased by Worcester City Council in 1921 and from then until the late 1960s, it was the School Clinic. In 1971 Tudor House became a branch of Worcester City Museum, showing displays relating to the social history of the city. Many museum visitors though, still remember vividly childhood visits to the school dentist!

46. The corner of Edgar Street and College Street, from Sidbury, a photograph taken in about 1924. Superficially, little has changed from when this view was taken. Holloway's building on the corner still remains, but the White Hart has been rebuilt. The large warehouse/depository which dominates the right hand side of the photograph is now an annexe of Worcester Technical College.

THE COMMANDERY, WORCESTER.
PUBLISHED BY JOSEPH LITTLEBURY

47. The Commandery in Sidbury, pictured in a postcard published by Littlebury's Press, which owned the building from 1905 until it was purchased by the city in 1973 for use as a museum. Founded as the hospital of St. Wulstan in the thirteenth century, the Commandery stood outside the city walls. The surviving buildings date from the fifteenth century. At the time of the Civil War, when the Commandery was the Royalist headquarters at the Battle of Worcester (1651), it was the home of the Wylde family, wealthy cloth merchants. From the mid-eighteenth century the Commandery went into a decline under a succession of owners, one of whom removed the walls of the magnificent Great Hall to form the carriageway clearly visible in the photograph. The Littlebury family eventually restored the hall to its original proportions.

48. The Commandery from the Sidbury side, in another of Littlebury's published views. The Great Hall runs across the picture with its carriageway behind the iron gate. The original entrance, later reinstated by Littlebury's, was to the left of the carriageway. Notice that all of the timber framing on the Great Hall has had its original infill replaced with brick.

49. St Peter's Street and Church in the 1890s. A church had stood on this spot since at least 969 A.D. At first dedicated to St. Perpetua and St. Felicitas, it became St. Peter's in 1420 and its parish was outside the city walls. With the removal of the walls and development of the city outside their boundary, the parish expanded rapidly. The church shown in the postcard was built in 1836-1838. The medieval houses of St. Peter's Street and adjoining King Street were demolished in the slum clearances of the 1930s. St. Peter's Church itself was knocked down in 1976 and today only the wall of the rectory remains.

50. Looking back at the Cross from Foregate, in a view posted in August 1912. The façade of Anderson and Virgo, the chemists, remained virtually unchanged until the shop ceased trading in about 1980. Next door, on the corner of St. Nicholas Street, is The Public Benefit Boot Company, later and better known as Lennards. The company was established at the turn of the century and operated until the early 1970s. The beauty of St. Nicholas' Church is well demonstrated in this view and one can also see the double flight of steps which once formed the entrance to the church.

51. The Foregate, photographed in the late 1890s. On this spot stood one of the nine gateways through the medieval city wall. Sansome Street, going off to the right of this photograph, was originally called 'Town Ditch' since it followed the line of the defensive ditch. A workhouse for the parish of St. Nicholas was built here in 1699, which in 1731 became Worcester's Hopmarket. It was soon the most important hopmarket in the kingdom. In 1900 work began on demolishing these old buildings and replacing them with the splendid new premises which remain to this day, even though the Hopmarket has long ceased to function as such. The building on the left of the photograph, with clock and barometer just visible on the corner, is hardly changed today.

52. The Foregate, photographed on a miserable wet day in 1902 by T. Bennett of Broad Street, with only a road sweeper for company! A transitional stage in the reconstruction of the façades is shown. The Hopmarket appears to be completed, to the design of architect A.B. Rowe, resplendent in its terracotta. The premises of the National Provincial Bank still jut out and are awaiting being set back on the same line. Anderson & Virgo, a much loved Worcester chemist's shop, was in business in the Foregate from the 1850s until the 1970s.

53. A sale day in the Hopmarket, probably in the late 1890s, before it was rebuilt in its present form. At Worcester's Hop Fair, traditionally held on 19th September, surplus hops were sold off to dealers from all over the country. At this time, around 50,000 'pockets' of hops were sold each year at the Hopmarket.

54. Foregate Street as depicted on a postcard of about 1905. On the left is the Star Hotel, one of Worcester's early coaching inns, originally called the Star and Garter. From the Star and Garter and the Hop Pole next door, stage coaches departed frequently for various parts of the country. The spread of railways put an end to the stage coaches and by a strange twist of fate, the railway line from Worcester to Hereford passes beside the Star Hotel and across Foregate Street by its 'handsome iron bridge', opened in 1860.

55. Foregate Street decorated for the Coronation of King George V and Queen Mary in 1911. This view looking southwards towards the Cross, shows the Star Hotel on the right of the street, heavily emblazoned with bunting and garlands. Next to it is the sweet shop of John Sigley, who operated several outlets around the city for his confectionery factory in Carden Street. Next door again, are the premises of Henry Coombs, an old established Worcester auctioneer and valuer, who had moved around the corner from Shaw Street in 1910.

56. A closer look at the Foregate Street railway bridge, as refurbished in 1909 and with the addition of heraldic devices. Marks and Spencer's Penny Bazaar, adjacent to the bridge, opened in 1908 and was there until 1927 when it moved to the High Street. Through the arch of the bridge behind the trampole can be seen the Empire Music Hall, opened on the site of the old Foregate Hall in 1909. It became the Silver Cinema in 1915, which featured an opulent ballroom at first floor level.

57. The Shire Hall in Foregate Street was completed in 1838 to a design by Charles Day of Worcester, to house new County Courts and Judges' Lodgings, replacing those at the Guildhall, which were deemed to be inadequate. This photograph was probably taken to show the statue of Queen Victoria, sparkling white and brand new in Carrara marble, which was unveiled in 1890 to commemorate the Queen's Golden Jubilee of 1887. The statue was the work of Thomas Brock, the Worcester sculptor, whose best-known work, for which he was knighted in 1911, is the Victoria Memorial in front of Buckingham Palace. In the foreground of the picture the horse tram rails can be seen.

58. The Shire Hall and the Victoria Institute in about 1898. The Victoria Institute was built specially to combine the Library and Museum, and the School of Art and Science under one roof. The cost was met partly out of the proceeds of the Worcestershire Exhibition of 1882 and partly from donations made by local philanthropists. The architects were John Simpson and Milner Allen. The Duke of York (later George V) laid the foundation stone for the new Victoria Institute on 3rd April 1894 and it was declared open by Lady Mary Lygon on 1st October 1896. Note the cabmen's rest hut.

59. Acacia House (on the right) and 26-27 Foregate Street, photographed during the early 1890s. This rare photograph shows the houses that were demolished to build the Victoria Institute (now the City Library and Museum). Construction work began in 1894, with the rubble from the original houses forming the foundations of the new building.

60. The opening morning of the new Secondary School for Girls in Taylor's Lane, 2nd November 1910. The School had its origins in the Victoria Institute Mixed School, housed in the Institute's Technical School Annexe in Sansome Walk. In 1908 the Mixed School was disbanded, the boys transferring to the Grammar School. The Secondary School for Girls later moved to Barbourne and then to Spetchley. It was redesignated the Worcester Grammar School for Girls in 1944 and closed in 1984.

61. Gregory's Grocery store in the Tything, in a photograph dating from 1908. Gregory's was in business from the turn of the century until the 1930s. The care and pride taken over the arrangement of the goods in the window display is very apparent and typical of the small shopkeepers of the period. The prices of the goods make interesting reading, bearing in mind that the average working man's wage was 22/- (£1.10) a week.

62. This postcard, sent in 1928, depicts the frontage of 'Britannia House' in the Upper Tything, now the Alice Ottley School for Girls. Dating from about 1730 the house was designed by the local architect Thomas White, also responsible for the Guildhall. During the 1860s, Britannia House became a boys' school and in 1883, the Worcester High School for Girls. The title was changed to the Alice Ottley School in 1914 in honour of its first headmistress who died in 1912.

63. The Royal Grammar School, Worcester, in the Upper Tything, from a postcard issued during the mid-1920s. With its origins dating back at least to the thirteenth century, the Grammar School was chartered by Queen Elizabeth I in 1561. The school at that time was located next to St. Swithun's Church in a small hall which still survives. It was moved to the Upper Tything site in 1868. In the foreground is the 'Old School' building, designed by A.E. Perkins, who also restored the Cathedral fabric.

64. The new 'Physical Laboratory' of the Royal Grammar School, Worcester, opened in 1922, from the same set of postcards as the previous view.

65. An aerial view of Barbourne Road taken in 1929, with, at its centre, the new Secondary School for Girls, opened that year and built on the site of Thames House. Facing the school across Barbourne Road is St. George's Square, a development dating from the 1830s, at the head of which is St. George's Church, built to the design of Sir Aston Webb in 1894 to replace an earlier church. The roofs of the St. George's Laundry (demolished 1985) are to the left of the church. In the top right hand corner of the picture is Barbourne Brewery, founded in 1851 and associated from 1885 until the late 1960s with the Spreckley family. The malt house of the brewery still survives, converted to housing.

66. Standard 4 Boys' Class of St. George's School, photographed in about 1890. St. George's Chapel School, opened in 1833, was the first Church of England 'Parish' School in Worcester and was part of the 'National School' System. In 1855 only one in eight children attended school, but the 1870 Education Act satisfied the growing demand for a complete Elementary Education supported by 'the rates'. Under its dual system denominational schools such as St. George's, were allowed to continue as 'Voluntary Schools' whilst School Boards, undenominational and supported by grants, fees and rates, were set up to operate schools where none had previously existed. Worcester's School Board established six elementary schools in its thirty-year existence.

67. A class at Red Hill School, photographed at the turn of the century. Red Hill, or St. Mary's as it was officially called, was one of the schools operated by Worcester's School Board set up as a result of the Elementary Education Act of 1870. The others were Hounds Lane (near All Saint's Church), St. Martin's, St. Barnabas, Comer Gardens and Cherry Orchard. At first limited to teaching the 'three Rs', the School Boards were from 1891 allowed to widen the curriculum with drawing, cookery, woodwork and singing. The Boards were abolished in 1902 and in its last report Worcester School Board was able to announce that 'the School Life of the children is now not only healthful and happy, but is spent amidst surroundings at once refined and elevating, and infinitely superior to the homes from which many of the children come'.

68. This extremely rural view, dating possibly from the 1870s, shows Barbourne Road looking north. Barbourne Brook crosses beneath the bridge in the centre of the picture. On the left hand side of the road was an eighteenth century house with 18 acres of private park on which was established in 1883, Barbourne College, a boys' school. It became Gheluvelt Park in the 1920s as Worcester's Great War Memorial, named after the Flemish village where the Worcestershire Regiment made an heroic charge in October 1914.

69. Barbourne water tower, to the north of Pitchcroft, was a landmark until the early 1960s, when it was demolished. It originally formed a vital component of the city's waterworks, built in 1770 to replace an earlier works near the river bridge. A waterwheel lifted water from the River Severn to the top of the tower, from where the city was supplied by a basic system of wooden pipes. In 1810 the waterworks was moved to North Quay where a steam pump lifted water through cast iron pipes to a large iron reservoir situated in the Trinity, from whence it was supplied to customers twice a week via standpipes. The water tower was eventually converted into dwellings.

70. A pleasure boat heading upriver towards Bevere Lock in about 1910. Pitchcroft and the racecourse are on the right bank of the river. Pitchcroft was originally a system of small fields and orchards, with gravel pits at its northern end. Horse racing on it began during the early eighteenth century and until 1880 was over natural fences. The grandstand seen on the postcard, was erected in 1823 and included an hotel. It was operated by a local charity, St. Oswald's Hospital, until the city bought it out in 1897, two years after purchasing Pitchcroft itself. The original grandstand was demolished in 1974.

71. The 'Dog and Duck' Ferry, from a postcard sent in 1910. Situated near the northern end of Pitchcroft, the ferry crossed to a waterman's tavern and a small quay, originally built to serve the outlying district of Martley. Sailing vessels would offload cargoes of hay and coal. The name of the public house — Dog and Duck — is believed to derive from a sport engaged in by watermen, in which dogs were trained to retrieve flightless ducks from the river.

72. A balloon ascent from Pitchcroft, one of the local events to celebrate the coronation of King George V in 1911. The houses in the background are Severn Terrace, and looming over them, between the chimneys, can be seen the top of the County Gaol in Castle Street. Balloons and pioneer aircraft ascents were popular attractions on Pitchcroft; the first aeroplane demonstration taking place during the Agricultural Show on 11th June 1910. Unfortunately, lack of crowd control led to the aeroplane, an army Bleriot, killing a local woman and injuring five others with its propellor. Despite this, aeroplane ascents continued and the celebrated aviators, Colonel S.F. Cody and Gustav Hamel, flew from Pitchcroft during the next three years.

73. The Infirmary from Pitchcroft, in a postcard view from the turn of the century. Apart from horse-racing, Pitchcroft had long been used as a location for travelling fairs and circuses and for training by local volunteer military units. In 1895, the City Corporation purchased Pitchcroft in several lots and paid £1,000 to extinguish its Commonable Rights. In 1899, the mayor, Lord Beauchamp, presented the ornamental gates which still exist, seen in the centre of the picture. On the left of the photograph are the turrets of the County Gaol and the spire of the Presbyterian Church (demolished in 1964), both in Castle Street. The more distant spire is that of St. Mary's Church in Sansome Walk. Notice the Infirmary Chapel, almost screened by the trees.

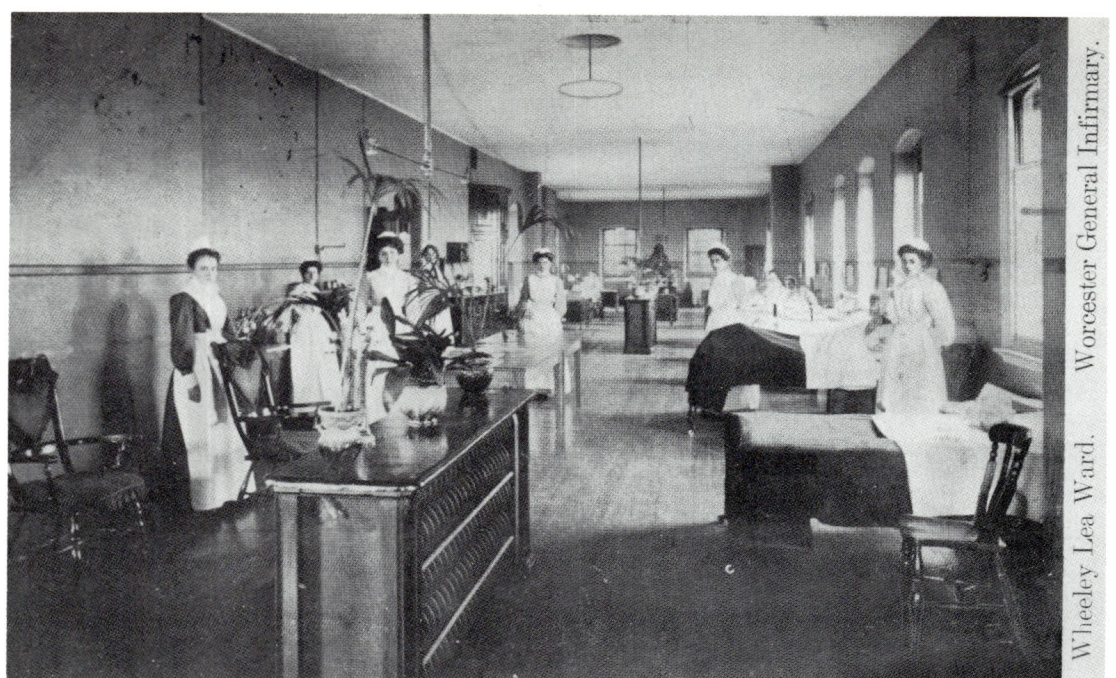

74. Wheeley-Lea Ward, Worcester General Infirmary, in a picture postcard sent in 1907. Worcester's Infirmary was established in 1745 in a rented house in Silver Street, close to Lowesmoor. As a voluntary hospital, it was one of a very small number outside London. Demands on the Infirmary led to the construction of a new building, completed in 1771 at the lower end of Salt Lane, now called Castle Street. The 1771 building still exists in the midst of later additions and extensions. In 1832, Worcester's distinguished physician, Sir Charles Hastings, founded, in the Board Room of the Infirmary, what was later to become The British Medical Association. A century later, in 1932, following a visit by H.R.H. The Prince of Wales, the General Infirmary was permitted to use the title 'Worcester Royal Infirmary'.

75. The County Gaol in Castle Street, 1927. The County's House of Correction was situated in the old medieval castle, adjacent to the Cathedral, until 1813, despite outbreaks of 'gaol fever' in 1788 which led to the condemnation of the accommodation. In 1813 the brand new County prison in Salt Lane was completed. Built in the style of a medieval fortress (in memory of its predecessor?), the County Gaol's presence led to the rechristening of Salt Lane as Castle Street. Originally the prison had ninety cells, but a further eighty were added in 1839, at the height of the 'Chartist' agitation. Debtors were housed in the County Gaol until 1873 and until 1863, executions within its walls were held in public. The Infirmary, just across the road, often received the bodies for dissection. The last execution took place within the County Gaol in 1919 and it was closed in 1928. For a time it was used as temporary housing for the homeless. The façade was demolished during the late 1930s, but several cell blocks remained until 1987.

76. Worcester was for many centuries an important market town for livestock brought in from the pastures to the west and north of the city. Traditionally, cattle markets were held in the streets right up until the early nineteenth century, All Saints' being the major location. The obvious inconveniences of such practise led to attempts to harness animal trading and, finally, in 1836, a purpose-built cattle market opened at the lower end of the Butts, part of which site it still occupies today. The photograph dates from 1908. In the background is the viaduct of the Worcester to Hereford railway line.

77. Broad Street, Worcester, in a postcard of about 1905, looking back towards the Cross. Broad Street has long been an important commercial street. During late medieval times, it was the location for the sheep market, vital to a city whose wealth was based on the wool trade. The street was given a boost by the opening of the new river bridge in 1781 and two large coaching inns were situated in it — the Crown and the Bell. In 1825 a Broad Street chemists' partnership, Messrs. Lea & Perrins, began production of their 'Worcestershire Sauce' at the rear of the shop — the rest, as they say, is history!

78. An advertisement for the long-established and well-loved Beard's greengrocery at 4-5 Broad Street. It was in operation from about 1910 until 1970.

79. The Bell Hotel in Broad Street was one of Worcester's coaching inns originally, with a history dating back into the eighteenth century. It stood across what is now Angel Place, with a narrow alleyway, Little Angel Street, beside it, running through to Angel Street. In 1912, the Bell Hotel was demolished and Angel Place was formed.

80. The other side of the story – the rear of the Bell Hotel showing the stables and Little Angel Street, with, on the far right hand side, the façade of Lewis Clarke's Brewery.

81. The Theatre Royal, Angel Street, in about 1925 from a photograph by W.W. Dowty. Worcester's 'legitimate' theatre (there have also been several music halls and 'concert halls') first opened in 1780 and adopted the title 'Royal' in 1805. It was twice destroyed by fire and rebuilt, the second time in 1912. During the latter half of the nineteenth century, it housed some spectacular and expensive productions, but like most provincial theatres, it could not combat cinema and later radio and television. It went into a slow decline, finally staging shoddy touring 'variety' shows and eventually closing in 1955. It was demolished in 1959 and a supermarket now stands in its place. The new Swan Theatre in The Moors opened in 1965.

82. Bridge Street from the river end, in a postcard view of about 1910. Bridge Street was part of the river bridge development carried out during the 1770s-1780s by John Gwynne. It was built on the ruins of a slum area called Rush Alley, and comprised houses of great elegance, although by the time of this postcard, many shop frontages had been added. On the right of the picture is the 'Bridge Inn'.

83. The river bridge from Bridge Street, in a view probably dating from 1912-1914. The iron balustrades of the bridge and its approaches, dating from the 1847 widening, can be plainly seen, as can the two domed tollhouses, on the far (St. John's) side. Wilesmith's timber yard can be seen on what became Cripplegate Park in 1932. In the same year the 'new' river bridge was opened, the main reason for which was the increase in road traffic crossing it. In this view however, there is little evidence of it, even though it was taken on a working day!

84. Although it looks like a film set for a Charles Dickens story, almost unbelievably, this photograph was taken in Worcester in about 1930. It shows Court No. 4 Newport Street, virtually in the city centre. It was taken by A.D. McGuirk for the city's Chief Sanitary Inspector, as a record of areas due for slum clearance. The houses are in effect medieval and the housing conditions inside them are best imagined. Large areas of the old city centre were 'cleared' between the 1920s and 1940s.

85. The line of Dolday is now largely lost to redevelopment. It ran from the west or lower end of Broad Street down to North Quay and leading off it was a series of courts, around which were miserable dwellings and lodging houses. In this view, taken in 1931 by A.D. McGuirk for the City Sanitary Inspector, one is looking down Dolday towards North Quay, where can be seen the Watermen's Church, built in 1859 to replace a converted barge. Church and most of Dolday were demolished during the 1940s.

86. Another view of Dolday, taken in 1931 by A.D. McGuirk, this time looking up Dolday towards the Broad Street end. On the left hand side of the picture, the whitewashed entrance leads through to No. 4 Court.

87. A postcard from about 1930 showing South Quay, with behind the warehouses, at the left, the tower of All Saints' Church; in the centre, Hounds Lane School, built by Worcester School Board in 1871 and at the right, St. Andrew's Church. The area on the right has been cleared of some of the 'slum dwellings' as witnessed by the open area around St. Andrew's.

88. St. Andrew's Church, photographed at the end of the last century. St. Andrew's was demolished in 1947, but the medieval tower with its spire, added in 1751 by the Worcester stonemason Nathaniel Wilkinson, still remains, famed as 'the Glovers' Needle'. St. Andrew's was once a highly respectable parish, but during the nineteenth century it declined, becoming a warren of squalid courts and tenement blocks. At the foot of the church can be seen 'The Wherry', a favourite haunt of watermen, closed in 1923. The warehouse in the left foreground still stands on South Quay. Sheppard's was one of many mineral water manufacturers which operated in Worcester, South Quay being one of the favoured locations for the industry. Sheppard's was in business from circa 1870 to 1900.

89. A view taken from the spire of St. Andrew's Church in the late 1920s, looking across the area known as Birdport. The street running out of the right hand side of the picture, is Powick Lane, which adjoined Bank Street. In the distance, at the top edge of the photograph can be seen, in the left hand corner, Lewis Clarke's Brewery; in the centre, the roofs of the Scala Cinema and the Theatre Royal; and towards the right hand corner, the Crown Hotel in Broad Street (the white building). The line of the road in the foreground was altered during the 1940s and renamed 'Deansway'. Most of the buildings in the foreground were lost to redevelopment during the 1960s and Crowngate now occupies the site, but the cottages in the bottom right hand corner survive as the Elgar School of Music.

90. Copenhagen Street, photographed from St. Andrew's Church spire in about 1930. This photograph clearly demonstrates the almost medieval, overcrowded conditions still prevalent in the city centre at that time. Cooken Street, as it was originally named, was the main thoroughfare to the quayside from the city centre. It was rechristened Copenhagen Street after Lord Nelson's famous naval victory, following his visit to Worcester in 1803. Just off the top left hand corner of the picture were the 'Model Dwellings' in St. Alban's Square, a mid-Victorian attempt to provide improved housing for the poor. The whole of this area was cleared during the 1930s and 1940s and the carpark of the Technical College now occupies the spot.

91. A fascinating photograph, dating from about 1920, of Birdport, now part of Deansway. Leading out of the left hand side of the picture, is Bull Entry, which took one up towards the High Street. On the far side of Bull Entry is Webb's Horsehair Factory, established in 1865 by Edward Webb for the production of high-quality horsehair carpets, the main customers for which were the railway companies, which needed them for their carriages. The whole of this area has now been lost to redevelopment.

FISH STREET, WORCESTER—Showing the old Fishmongers' Hall, built in the 15th century and demolished in 1906.
(From a Water Colour Drawing by E. A. Phipson.)

92. Fish Street, one of Worcester's oldest streets, was formerly Corviser Street, the centre for Worcester's leather trade, and is shown here in a postcard view by the artist E.A. Phipson, dated 1893. As its current name suggests, Fish Street was from the sixteenth century the location for fish sellers, but a 'Fishmongers' Hall' stood there from the thirteenth century. The hall in the foreground of the picture, built during the fifteenth century, was demolished in 1906. Fish from the river was an important part of the staple diet of Worcester people until the latter half of the last century, when navigational improvements, the construction of reservoirs in the Welsh headlands and industrial pollution of the Severn caused the decline of fish numbers. At the same time though, the growth of railways made sea fish readily available.

93. Let's take a closer look at Worcester's trams, very much part of the city scene for almost forty years. The horse tram system commenced in 1881 with three routes: from the Cross to the Portobello Inn, Bransford Road; from the Cross to the Vine Inn, Ombersley Road and from St. Nicholas Street to Shrub Hill Railway Station. The tram depot was in the Bull Ring, St. Johns. In 1893, the system was taken over by a new company – Worcester Tramways Ltd –, which updated the system with double deck, two horse powered cars. In 1898, the British Electric Traction Co. acquired an interest in the business, which was retitled the Worcester Electric Traction Company and this photograph dates from about this year. Probably taken on a busy Saturday afternoon, it shows two of the fleet of seven double deck cars, with one of the two single deck 'toastrack' cars behind. On the left is one of the company's eleven horse buses which provided links with outlying suburbs and villages.

94. The last day of the Worcester Horse Tramways, Sunday 25th June 1903, with a specially posed commemorative photograph, taken outside the Tram Depot in the Bull Ring, St. Johns. On the right of the picture, standing in front of the tramcar emerging from the depot, are the two inspectors (wearing bowler hats) with between them the Manager of the Tramways from 1894 to 1908, R.R. Fairbairn, who was later Mayor of Worcester and also its Member of Parliament. The three boys on the left of the upper deck of the other tramcar are his sons.

Worcester Electric Tramway Siege, 1903-4.

T. Bennett & Sons, Photographers, Worcester and Malvern.

95. Electrification of the tramway system took place during the winter of 1903-1904. Work caused such considerable disruption of the city centre, coincidental with a spell of extremely wet weather, that streets were for a time completely impassable! Celebrated as the 'Worcester Electric Tramway Siege' the event was commemorated in a set of postcards issued by T. Bennett & Son of Broad Street. This view shows the scene in the Cross, looking northwards.

96. Another from the 1904 'Tramway Siege' postcard set, this time showing the laying of the track out across the river bridge. The gauge of the track was 3 feet 6 inches and the tramway system covered some 5.75 miles. For most of its length it was single line with passing places for the tramcars. Double line sections included the Cross and High Street, Lowesmoor, London Road and the river bridge.

97. A postcard view of the Cross, the original of which was handtinted, showing to perfection the overhead electricity supply for the tram system. The trams were the biggest single customer of the City of Worcester Electricity Works, originally established at Powick Bridge, but replaced by a new, larger power station in 1903, located in Hylton Road. Dissatisfaction with the tramway system began during the 1920s, as the amount of motor traffic rapidly increased and trams were believed to hamper its flow. The system was closed on 31st May 1928 and public transport in the city was leased to the Midland Red motor bus company.

98. Tramcars Nos. 3 and 5 in the Cross; a photograph taken right at the start of the electric tram service in 1904. The cars look to be in pristine condition and without the large number of advertisements which they soon carried. It would appear that work on the overhead system has not yet been completed either.

99. The electric tramcar service commenced on 6th February 1904. As well as the old horse tram routes to St. Johns (extended along Malvern Road), Ombersley Road and Shrub Hill, the electric trams went from the Cross to Astwood Road Cemetery, London Road and Bath Road. The entire system extended 5.75 miles. Fifteen open-topped cars were operated, in a smart Brunswick green and cream livery. Two extra cars were added in 1922. The photograph shows Car No. 6 with its crew. Their uniform was dark blue with red piping on trousers, jacket and cap. Buttons and badge were brass. Note the 'motorman's' canvas weathershield.

100. The tram depot was in St. Johns, on the corner of the Bull Ring and Henwick Road. This photograph, taken in about 1904, shows from left to right: the inspection pit; a tower wagon for repairs to the overhead supply; a horse-drawn char-à-banc and behind the two tramcars, the paint shop. Workshop benches stood along the right hand wall.

101. A horse tram crossing the river bridge and entering New Road, towards the end of the 1890s. On the right hand side is one of the bridge tollhouses which were demolished during the 1920s. The bridge, which cost £30,000 in 1781, was chiefly paid for by tolls levied on all passengers, whether on foot or in vehicles. By 1809, the debt was reduced to £5,000 and the toll on foot passengers ceased. The bridge finally became free on 1st January 1828. Behind the tram, on the corner of Bridge Street and South Quay, is a sign for Stretton & Co's Worcestershire Sauce, one of the very many companies then producing sauces similar to Lea & Perrins' product.

102. The extensive timber yard of J. Wilesmith on Hylton Road just prior to the First World War. Wilesmith's was established in Bath Road in about 1810 and the Hylton Road yard was in operation until the creation of Cripplegate Park in 1930. The office building in the centre of the picture still survives, however. Note that Wilesmith's made full use of the River Severn as a means of transport — timber was always an important cargo on the river. On the left of the photograph, the approach to the river bridge can be seen, along with its two tollhouses. The photograph is by Horace Dudley of Broad Street.

103. Tybridge Street, St. Johns, photographed in 1927. Originally known as Cripplegate, this area was made up of crowded and squalid courts of mean houses, interspersed with public houses and 'light industry', mainly involved with the river. Soon after this photograph was taken, Cripplegate was cleared and a children's playground now occupies the whole area of the photograph.

104. St. Clement's Church, Henwick Road, from a picture postcard of about 1910. St. Clement's originally stood on the east bank of the river, near the medieval river bridge. It was possibly a Saxon church, but was rebuilt several times and was always liable to flooding. St. Clement's was a small parish and many of its users came from the suburb of St. Johns. In 1822 it was decided to build the new church on the west side of the river. It is an early example of the neo-Norman style. In the foreground of the picture runs the Worcester to Hereford railway line. Just beyond the level crossing, off to the right of the photograph, stood Henwick station, opened in 1859.

105. St. Johns, or St. John in Bedwardine, to give its full name, was a separate community which was brought within the city boundary only in 1837, and then just the area of the church and the Bull Ring. The remainder has been added to the city since. This postcard, one of a set taken on a snowy day in about 1910, shows the twelfth century church of St. John. The vicarage standing in front of it is a seventeenth century timber-framed building beneath its façade. The small octagonal building belonged to a weighbridge. On the right hand side can be seen the Angel Inn with its large lamp and in the foreground, the boot and shoe shop (1 of 3) of the Noake Brothers, whose business was established in Barbourne in about 1800, and who claimed to be the largest manufacturer of hand-sewn boots in the county.

106. Another view from the 'St. Johns in the snow' set of about 1910, this time showing Vernon Park Road from across Malvern Road. The houses in the Vernon Park Estate were built between 1900 and 1908.

107. From the end of the last century, to take a trip on a steamer from Worcester was an extremely popular pastime during the summer months and several companies, perhaps the best known of which were Everton and Roberts, operated pleasure boats. Trips upriver to Stourport and downriver to Tewkesbury were usual and boats from both of those places were also frequently seen in Worcester. The photograph, which dates from just before the First World War, shows steamers loading at North Quay. Behind them is the hop warehouse belonging to Firkins and Co. and the public house called 'The Old Rectifying House', then operated by the Worcester brewer Lewis, Clarke & Co., whose brewery was in Angel Place. 'The Rectifying House' was originally part of a distillery which occupied the site and rectifying of spirits was carried out in it. The façade of the building dates from the 1880s.

108. In this view of 1918, North Quay is shown on the left, along with some of the many pleasure boats of all sizes which were so popular for outings from the turn of the century.

109. The elegant pleasure steamer 'My Queen', pictured at South Quay with a party of trippers, in about 1900. The buildings along South Quay indicate the diverse commercial activity to be found there. Whitehouse's iron warehouse was established in about 1895 and was in business until 1915. The Sauce Works on the right was operated by Messrs. Waldron & Co., one of the many competitors to Lea & Perrins. Notice the tiny tea-rooms squeezed in between the warehouses!

110. 'The Sebright Arms' in London Road, still a popular public house on the south-east side of the city. The landlady at the time this photograph was taken in the mid-1890s, was Mrs. Emily Williams, formerly of the Crown Inn, on Tallow Hill. Mrs. Williams brewed her own ale, according to the notice above the pub entrance.

111. A terrace of houses in Wyld's Lane, photographed for a postcard of about 1912 to 1914. A typical speculative development of the turn of the century, built to attract the lower middle class purchaser or tenant. For his money, the customer got a sturdy dwelling with its own individual name above the door and a front garden, albeit tiny, with iron railings and a gate. Lavatory facilities however, would still have been outside the back door!

112. The archetypal corner shop, J.A. Fosbury's Grocery on the corner of Wyld's Lane and Park Street, photographed by G. Colwell of London Road in about 1910. The Fosbury family's association with the shop lasted from the early 1880s until the 1950s and happily, despite decades of changing habits in shopping, this is one particular corner shop that is still going strong!

113. Little Park Street and Beaver Row, photographed in 1926, complete with some of their residents. These streets near to Wyld's Lane were typical examples of nineteenth century speculative building at a time of industrial growth. During the 1920s, the City Council refurbished many of them and this photograph is of improved housing. Little Park Street and Beaver Row were demolished during the 1950s.

114. Worcester has been linked with the production of fine porcelain since the establishment of what was to become the Royal Worcester Porcelain Company in 1751. In the 1860s, James Hadley, widely reckoned to be the finest porcelain modeller of the nineteenth century, joined the Royal Worcester Company. In 1875 he left to work as a freelance designer and in 1896 he established his own manufactory in Diglis Road, shown in the photograph. Hadley did not compete with Royal Worcester, but produced his own highly individual range of art pottery. In 1903 James Hadley died. His three sons carried on the company for a while, but in 1905 they sold out to the Royal Worcester Company.

115. This photograph, specially posed, presumably for publicity purposes, shows the James Street premises of The Albion Box Company, formerly W. Aston's, in the area of the city known as the Blockhouse. The Albion Company's 'Reliance Works' reckoned to manufacture all sizes of wooden crate or box to order, and from the contents of the cart, they would appear to have had a sideline in firewood too! W. Aston also operated a factory at Diglis for the manufacture of broom handles etcetera, importing timber direct from Scandinavia. The photograph was taken in 1908.

116. In about 1855, W.B. Williamson, a Wolverhampton tinsmith, set up in Worcester to manufacture a wide range of articles in sheet steel and tinplate. His business prospered and in 1858 he opened his 'Providence Works' on the corner of Charles Street in the Blockhouse area of the city and, as a sideline, went into making tin canisters for soups and biscuits. Under W.B. Williamson's sons the canister business flourished, especially airtight tins for cigarettes, for which the company were the sole suppliers. Eventually during the 1930s, Williamson's became a part of the giant Metal Box Company combine. A new factory for tin cans was built, but the Providence Works continued to produce other lines — biscuit tins, oil cans and domestic ware — until 1963.

117. The construction of the Worcester and Birmingham Canal, opened in 1815, was a great spur to the development of new industry in the city. Along its banks, particularly in the Lowesmoor area, iron foundries and manufactories of all kinds sprung up. One of the ironfounders was Hardy and Padmore, established in 1814, which originally produced cooking ranges, firegrates and general ironmongery. Towards the end of the nineteenth century, Hardy and Padmore began to specialise in street furniture — lamp posts, benches, gratings, manhole covers, etcetera — many examples of which still survive all over Britain as well as abroad. The company ceased operation in 1967. The photograph, dating from 1903, shows a woodworking shop in which wooden patterns for the castings are being made.

118. Amongst the many industrial concerns which set up in the Lowesmoor area in the last century, was J.O. Brettell, the engineer, whose works was in Shrub Hill Road. He was established in about 1875 and continued in business until the early years of this century. Calling himself a 'general engineer', Brettell built iron bridges, roofs, tanks, boilers, water cranes, wagons and railway turntables and was also an iron and brass founder. Some of his splendid-looking workforce is pictured here at some time during the 1880s. Could the gentleman in the bowler hat standing at the rear of the group on the left be Mr. Brettell himself?

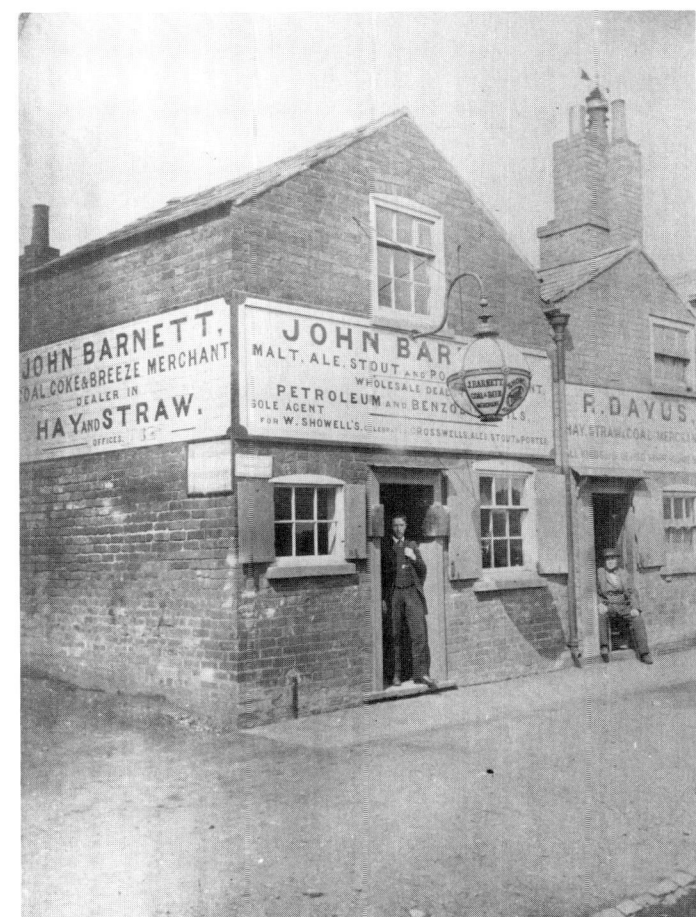

119. The premises of John Barnett, the corn and seed merchant, on Lowesmoor Wharf. Established in 1873, John Barnett occupied this building soon afterwards. Lowesmoor Basin was intended to be the Worcester terminus of the Worcester and Birmingham Canal, opened in 1815. Diglis Basins were an afterthought and were never completely a commercial success. Hay and straw, as well as coal, were the most usual cargoes for narrowboats serving Lowesmoor Basin at the end of the last century.

120. Shrub Hill Railway Station, a postcard from the turn of the century. 'Railway mania' first touched Worcester in 1840 with the opening of the local section of the Birmingham and Gloucester Railway. To save expense, the line by-passed the city with a station at Spetchley, served by a horse-bus link. Worcester was without a direct rail connection until 1853, when the Oxford, Worcester and Wolverhampton Railway opened. Its new station at Shrub Hill was completed in 1865 to a design by Edward Wilson. For a time Worcester was something of a local railway centre, since the O, W and W eventually also controlled the Worcester and Hereford line, before itself being absorbed by the Great Western Railway in 1863.

121. In 1864 the Worcester Engine Works Company Limited was established to construct railway locomotives and rolling stock and a huge, splendid works building was erected in Shrub Hill Road, to the design of the architect Thomas Dickson. Unfortunately, despite exporting a small number of locomotives, the company never really prospered and finally went into liquidation in 1871. A sad note, pencilled on the back of this photograph reads 'The last engine built at Shrub Hill', although this may not necessarily be true!

122. In 1882, the empty railway engine works was used to house 'The Worcestershire Exhibition', designed as a showcase for the county's historical treasures and industrial and artistic endeavours. The exhibition was a colossal success, some 250,000 visitors seeing it during its run of three months. Its profits were used to establish museums, libraries and other educational facilities in Worcestershire. The photograph shows Shrub Hill Road at the opening of the Worcestershire Exhibition on 18th July 1882. The official photographer to the Exhibition was Norman May of Malvern.

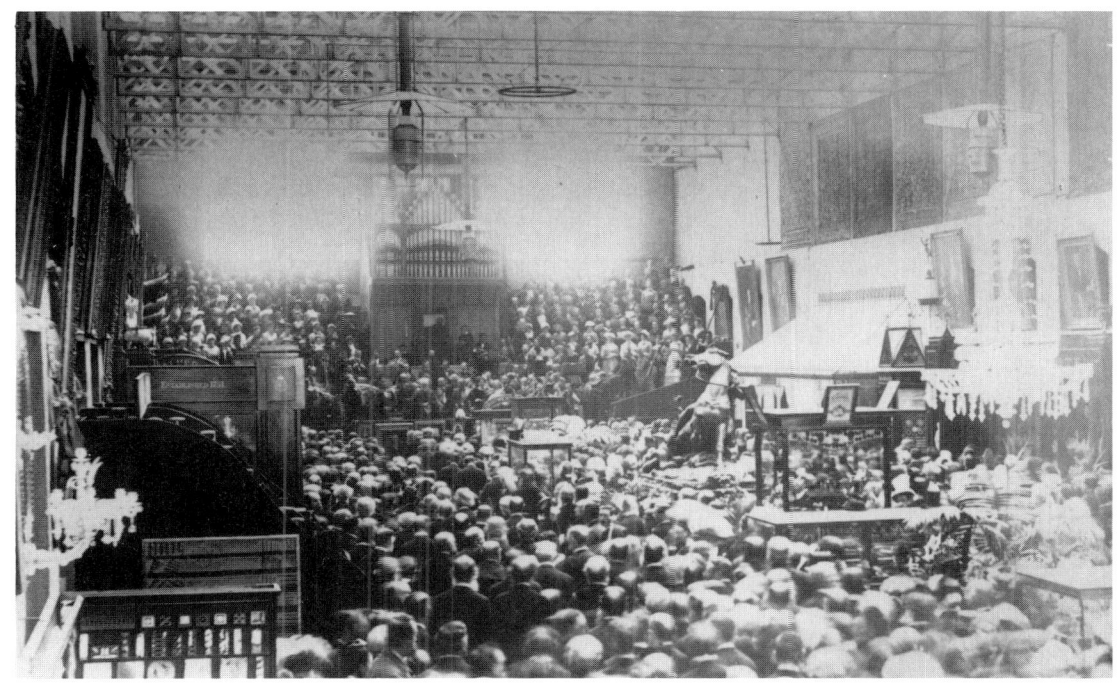

123. Following on from the previous photograph, this one shows the scene during the opening ceremony of the Worcestershire Exhibition on 18th July 1882. The central hall of the old engine works came to be known as the 'nave' during the course of the exhibition. Amongst the seated guests one can see display cases containing the wares of the county's major industries: Stourbridge glass, Dudley iron, Redditch needles, Droitwich salt and Worcester porcelain and gloves. Dominating the scene was the huge equestrian sculpture 'A Moment of Peril' by the Worcester sculptor Thomas Brock. On the walls were portraits gathered in from the great houses of the county, and higher still, rows of Kidderminster carpets. At the far end of the 'nave' can be seen the organ, specially removed from St. Mary Magdalene Church, and the chorus and full orchestra which opened the Exhibition with a performance of the Hallelujah Chorus, accompanied (from outside!) by a salute from the guns of the Volunteer Artillery.

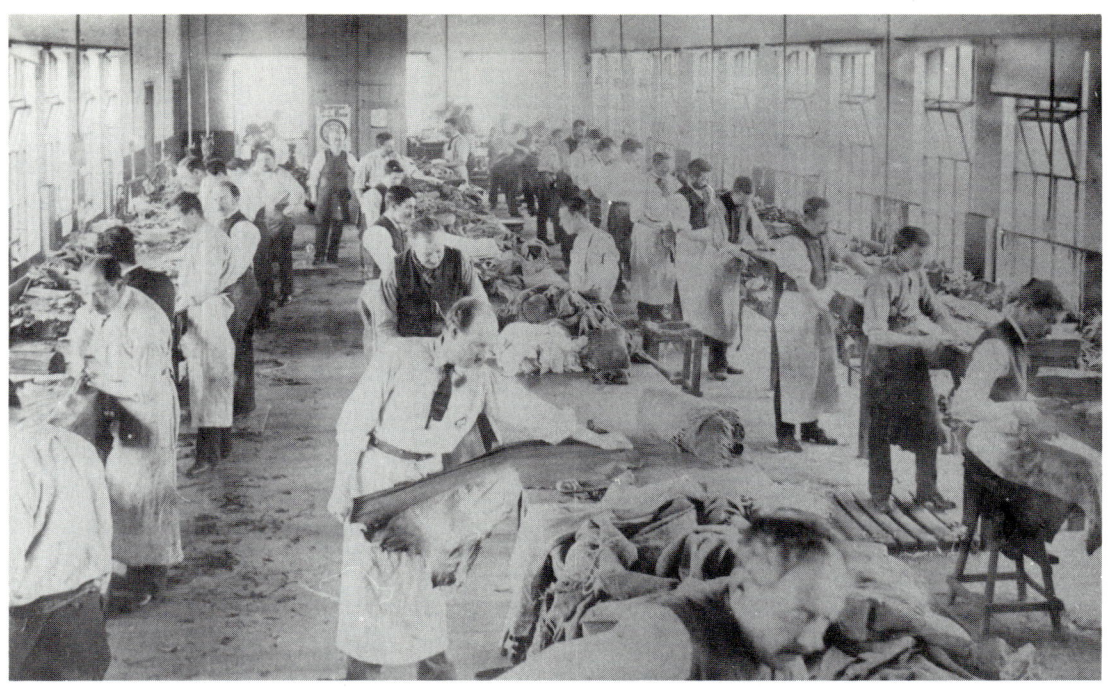

124. The leather glove industry, once pre-eminent in Worcester, was in slow decline from 1826, when import duties were removed from foreign gloves. The 108 glove manufacturers recorded in 1830, had fallen to a mere eleven by 1884. In that year however, there was a revival when the Fownes Company, established in Worcester during the eighteenth century, but moved away, returned to the city into a new purpose-built factory in Talbot Street. The photograph shows a cutting room in Fownes' factory in about 1895. On the centre bench the skins are being prepared by being wrapped in damp hessian cloth and then stretched, whilst the cutters work at the window benches.

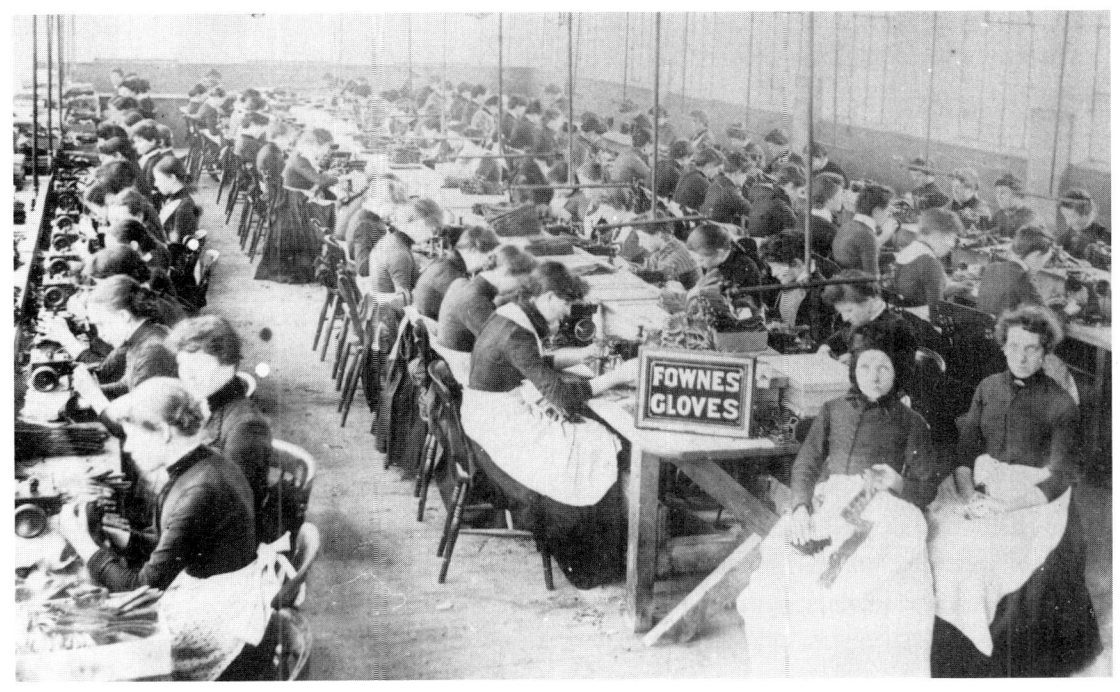

125. Another view from Fownes' Talbot Street factory in about 1890. This is a finishing shop where the women are making up the completed gloves by stitching the seams. Notice the open 'fishtail' type gas lights. Fownes' factory was in operation until the 1970s and can still be seen, now in use as an hotel, as a prominent landmark on the City Walls road.

126. It wasn't all work however, as witnessed by this splendid group photograph by T. Bennett, of the Fownes Cycling Club, taken in the rear yard of the factory in about 1899-1900. The large number of young women in the group bears testimony to the liberating influence of the bicycle. Not only did it give women temporary freedom from household drudgery or sewing machine, but it also freed them from the suffocating stuffiness of nineteenth century costume. Thanks to the bicycle, women's clothing became lighter and allowed freedom of movement, even if fashionable fads such as 'leg of mutton' sleeves still had to be followed! The original caption to this photograph, which must have been used for publicity purposes, says 'Some of the people who make and some of those who wear Fownes Gloves'.

127. The Co-operative movement began during the 1840s to combat high prices and bad practises in the selling of food and other necessities. In Worcester the first effort took place in the 1860s, involving railwaymen and Dent, Allcroft glovers. It failed, but valuable lessons were learned and in 1881 the Co-operative Baking Society was formed to provide cheap bread, originally from a bakery in Mealcheapen Street and then from the old Gaol's bakery in Union Street. Despite opposition from city bakers and millers, the Society began to prosper and was able to offer a good dividend to its members. In 1883, the Society built its first new bakery in Clare Street, adjacent to Fownes Glove Factory. It is shown in the photograph with its adjoining manager's house. By 1890 the 'Co-op' was able to offer drapery, boots, shoes and hardware from its shop in St. Nicholas Street.

128. The old skating rink, East Street, in the Arboretum circa 1900. The built-up area to the east of Foregate Street, known as the Arboretum, was originally Sansome Fields, a popular area for recreation. In 1840 the Worcester Public Pleasure Grounds Company was set up to develop the Fields and in 1859 it opened the 25 acres of pleasure grounds, in which were flower beds, terraces, fountains, a bowling green, a cricket pitch, a crystal pavilion for entertainments, a skating rink and an arboretum. Unfortunately, the pleasure grounds were financially unsuccessful and in 1868 the Company sold up the land for redevelopment as housing. The old skating rink remained, seen here as the warehouse of the Constance Hardware Company. In 1915 it became a bus garage and it was demolished in 1972.

129. Bartholemew's Baths in Sansome Walk, 1895. Charles Bartholemew was an exponent of water cures and medicinal baths and opened his Worcester Baths and Hydro in 1852, after travelling widely to study European techniques. Apart from the almost legendary 'bathing barges' on the river, the Sansome Walk Baths contained Worcester's only swimming pool. They continued in use, operated by the Parks family from 1890 until 1972, when the City Swimming Pool was built on the same spot. The original pool still exists as a sunken garden.

130. Perhaps the best remembered of Worcester's independent brewing companies was Lewis, Clarke and Co., situated in Angel Place, where the tower of the brewery, so close to the city centre, was a prominent landmark. Lewis, Clarke and Co. owned a large number of public houses in and around Worcester and maintained an immaculate fleet of drays for deliveries. In this photograph though, taken in about 1910, the wagons belong to the Midland Railway. Lewis, Clarke & Co. were founded in about 1895 and ceased brewing in 1970, after being taken over.

131. A char-à-banc on a day out during the mid-1920s and parked on North Quay. Behind it, one can see across the river to Hylton Road and the Worcester Electricity Generating Works. Worcester's first power station was opened at Powick Bridge in 1894, where it used the River Teme to drive turbines — a very early application of hydro-electric power. The coal-fired power station in the photograph was opened in 1903 to cope with increased demand, the tramway system being the biggest customer. It was enlarged in 1924 and totally rebuilt in 1943-1944. In the early 1980s, the power station was made redundant and demolished. For those interested in motor vehicles, the char-à-banc is a rebodied ex-War Department Crossley! The photograph is by W.W. Dowty.

132. The City of Worcester Electricity Works, in its extended form, officially opened on 29th May 1924. The photograph is taken in Tybridge Street looking towards the river. To cope with increasing demands, the electricity works was fitted with a 3,000 KW turbo-alternator, the turbines for which were driven by superheated steam. Feed water was from the river and the boilers were coal-fired. The photograph shows the improved coal-handling arrangements necessitated by the installation. Since the power station had no direct link with the railway, a fleet of steam wagons brought coal from the railside and dropped it into the 500 ton capacity pit seen on the end of the building. From there, the overhead traverser, fitted with a 1 ton grab, took the coal into the 100 ton bunkers fitted over the boilers. This arrangement lasted until the works was completely rebuilt in 1943-1944.

133. The entry of the City Electricity Works in the Worcester Carnival of 1927: 'The Megohms', a typical concert party! It's good to see that they were staunch supporters of electricity, for the lorry they have is a Tilling-Stevens petrol-electric vehicle, on which the engine powered a dynamo to turn the rear axle by means of an electric motor!

134. The delivery van of F.D. Jones, the baker of No. 1 Love's Grove, just off Castle Street, photographed in about 1910. A typical vehicle for deliveries in towns, many commercial concerns would have operated similar vans at the turn of the century. It is photographed outside one of the public houses of Lewis, Clarke & Co., the brewers, but it is difficult to ascertain which! F.D. Jones' were in business from 1902 until the middle of the 1920s.

135. With the decline in the glove industry during the nineteenth century, the tradition of leather working in Worcester was maintained by the setting up of several boot and shoe factories, the most significant of which was J.W. Willis, established in 1863 and trading from 1885 under the name 'Cinderella Shoes'. In 1909 Cinderella moved to a new factory in Watery Lane, St. Johns. The photograph, taken in 1926, shows boot and shoe components being cut by machines powered by overhead line shafting. Cinderella ceased trading in 1976.

136. An advertising postcard, circa 1925, of Frederick Winwood Ltd, removers and storers of furniture, established early last century and the occupier of six warehouses around the city at the time of the First World War. Like very many other removal businesses, Winwoods took the opportunity, after 1918, of motorising its fleet by purchasing cheap ex-army lorries!

137. The City of Worcester's first professional police force, eighteen strong and modelled on London's Metropolitan Police, was raised in 1833, replacing earlier systems of 'watchmen'. Headquarters were originally the City Gaol in Union Street, until a new station was built in Copenhagen Street – nice and handy for the unruly quayside areas! The first full-time detective was appointed in 1867, but policewomen did not appear until 1948. That was also the year in which the City Police relinquished their responsibility for operating the fire brigade, which had been formed to complement those of the insurance companies. The photograph shows a hand-pulled ladder and hose wagon, purchased in 1875.

138. In the winter of 1917-1918, during the First World War, Worcester citizens discovered at first hand the privations of total war, as long queues for foodstuffs, particularly meat, margarine and butter, became an everyday occurrence. In spring 1918, a national 'Grow More Food' Campaign was held and in March this display was staged in front of the Cathedral, with exhibited war weapons, including a captured German Rumpler C1 aeroplane, and a parade of Land Army girls.

139. The caption on this postcard reads: 'Worcester's Tank Bank.' The Mark IV Tank 'Julian' was part of the 'Grow More Food' Campaign display in front of the Cathedral in March 1918.

140. A view which could not have been left out of any collection of Worcester postcards! For many people this is the enduring image of the city, and the one of which countless thousands have been printed and sold. Many would say that the Worcestershire County Cricket Club's ground is the most picturesque in the world. There had been County 'sides' from early in the nineteenth century and the present club dates from 1865, but it was not until 1899 that Worcestershire was admitted to the first-class County Championship. At that time the County Ground was merely three hayfields, rented from the Dean and Chapter of the Cathedral. The postcard dates from about 1912.